CW01635160

Threads of Destiny

A Village Girl's Tale of Resilience and Transformation

MARIA BELL

OBA connections

THREADS OF DESTINY
A Village Girl's Tale of Resilience and Transformation

Maria Bell

Published by
O • B • A Connections Ltd.
Email: obaconnections@gmail.com
Telephone: +44 (0) 7984 260 508
Website: www.obaconnections.com

Text copyright © 2023 Maria Bell.

The moral right of the author has been asserted in accordance with the Copyright Designs and Patent Act 1988.

First published 2023.

ISBN: 978-1-7391071-2-3

All rights reserved. No part of this publication may be reproduced, stored in a retrieval system, or transmitted in any form or by any means electronic, mechanical, photocopying or otherwise, without the prior written consent of the publisher; short extracts may be used for review purposes.

Edited by PenWorks Ltd.
Telephone: +44 (0) 7376 071 921
info@penworksltd.com

Cover/book design by Imaginovation Ltd.

Printed in the United Kingdom.

Contents

Dedication

This book is dedicated to all those who have faced adversity with unwavering faith and unyielding courage. It is a tribute to the indomitable human spirit that refuses to be defined by circumstances and instead rises above them.

To the unsung heroes who have battled illness, loss, and hardship, this book is for you. May the stories within these pages serve as a reminder of your remarkable strength and resilience. Your determination and faith inspire us all.

I extend my deepest gratitude to the families, friends, and communities who have offered support and love. Your presence and compassion have provided solace and encouragement during the darkest moments. May this book stand as a testament to the power of unity and support in times of trial.

May these words ignite hope, instil courage and awaken the belief that there is light beyond the shadows. This book is dedicated to all those who refuse to let adversity define them, who choose to embrace the journey, and illuminate the path for others to follow.

I extend my deepest gratitude to the families, friends, and communities who have offered support and love, leaning on the power of prayer and trusting in God's plan.

May this book stand as a testament to the miraculous workings of God in our lives and the strength that comes from placing our faith in Him. May these words ignite hope, instil courage, and awaken the belief in the extraordinary power of faith and God's unfailing love.

Acknowledgements

I would like to begin by expressing my deepest gratitude to the Lord God for granting me the strength and inspiration to complete this book. Without His divine guidance and support, this endeavour would not have been possible.

I extend my heartfelt appreciation to my late father, Raphael, whose belief in me and constant encouragement pushed me to pursue excellence in all aspects of my life.

To my beloved son, Mario, your uplifting words have been a constant source of strength throughout this journey. Your belief in me has been a driving force behind my determination to overcome challenges and reach new heights.

I would like to pay tribute to my mentor, the late Christine Cobham, whose invaluable guidance and wisdom shaped my growth as a writer. Her influence continues to inspire and motivate me, even in her absence.

I am deeply grateful to the Queens' Dialysis Unit and the Royal London Transplant Team for their exceptional care and support during trying times. Their dedication and expertise played a vital role in my well-being and enabled me to pursue my passion for writing.

I would like to express my sincere thanks to my editor, Idowu Thomas-Elekwa, for her meticulous attention to detail and commitment to excellence. Your expertise and professionalism have transformed this book into its best version.

To the remarkable Unique Women group, I am incredibly thankful for the empowerment you have provided. Your support and camaraderie have been a source of strength and inspiration throughout my journey.

To my past and present church family, you have been a pillar of support and encouragement throughout my life. Your prayers, love, and guidance have been the driving force behind my resilience and determination. You have embraced me with open arms, providing a nurturing environment for me to grow spiritually and personally. Your belief in my story and unwavering encouragement to share it with the world have been instrumental in shaping this book.

Lastly, I want to express my heartfelt appreciation to all my family and friends who have been by my side, offering their love, encouragement, and belief in me. Your presence in my life has shaped me into the woman I am today, and I am forever grateful for your support.

Foreword

In our society, we often take our health for granted, assuming that our bodies will always function as they should. However, for those who have experienced serious health issues, this assumption is shattered. Chronic kidney disease is one such condition that can drastically alter a person's life, requiring constant medical attention and lifestyle changes to manage.

Within the pages of this biography, we have the privilege of delving into the life of Maria, a kidney patient who has confronted these challenges with determination. Through her words, we gain profound insight into the physical and emotional toll that chronic illness can exact, as well as the resilience and tenacity required to navigate life with such a condition.

Maria's story serves as a poignant reminder that although health struggles can be isolating, we are never truly alone in our experiences. By generously sharing her journey, Maria offers a beacon of hope and inspiration to others who may find themselves facing their own health battles. Her story stands as a testament to the indomitable power of the human spirit and the strength that emerges when we persevere through adversity.

I also salute Maria's tenacity in the place of prayer, which has deepened her walk with the Lord. Despite facing tremendous challenges, she has remained resolute in her faith and calling. While others might have been discouraged and turned away from their walk with the Lord, Maria's unyielding dedication has qualified her as a true Kingdom Midwife and Intercessor, setting an example worthy of admiration and emulation. Her steadfastness in the place of prayer demonstrates the transformative power of faith and the strength it provides in the face of adversity.

Pastor Oyinlola Bukky Akande
Co-Senior Pastor,
Shalom Life Changers Ministries International,
United Kingdom.

Introduction

Threads of Destiny: A Village Girl's Tale takes you on a captivating journey through the life of a young girl, highlighting the beauty, challenges, and triumphs that shape her destiny. In this heartfelt tribute, we witness the resilience and determination of a village girl as she navigates the complexities of family, education, and societal expectations. Her story serves as an inspiration, reminding us of the power of perseverance and the pursuit of dreams against all odds. Through the highs and lows, the young girl's journey in "Threads of Destiny" resonates with universal themes of hope, love, and the indomitable spirit that resides within each of us.

As you follow her path, you will be captivated by the small victories, the lessons learned through adversity, and the transformative power of self-discovery. Threads of Destiny invites you to embrace the threads of your own life, finding solace and inspiration in the shared experiences that unite us all. Step into the enchanting world of this village girl's tale and be reminded that within every individual lies a unique story waiting to be told, a destiny waiting to be realised.

Chapter 1

The Little Village

NESTLED AMIDST THE tropical beauty of Jamaica, in the quaint village of Roehampton, a captivating story unfolds. This village, with its breath-taking landscapes and vibrant culture, becomes the backdrop for a tale of resilience, love, and the intertwining threads of life. A place where the rhythm of daily life is harmoniously entwined with the natural wonders that surround it.

The air is filled with the sweet scent of tropical fruits and the gentle rustle of coconut trees' leaves. The villagers, known for their warm hospitality and vibrant spirit, create a tight-knit community that embraces both joy and challenges with strength. In this quaint village, there lived a hardworking farmer and his five daughters. Sadly, their mother was absent from their lives, but the farmer's love for his children knew no bounds. He toiled tirelessly to provide for them and ensure their well-being in the close-knit community.

At the age of five, one of the farmer's daughters embarked on her first day of school, accompanied by her older sister. Joy radiated from her as they walked hand in hand, but upon reaching the school, her excitement turned into tears. The compassionate teacher gently separated her from her sister and guided her inside, offering reassurance and support. In the afternoon, her sister returned to collect her, the bond between them unbroken. Curiosity about her mother stirred within the young girl's heart. Observing other children with their loving mothers, she yearned for her own. Eventually, the truth unfolded: her mother had run away, leaving an irreplaceable void in her life.

Barefooted, she embarked on her daily journey to school, finding solace in playful moments with other children along the edge of the bushes. Despite the absence of their mother, the farmer's house was a hub of activity, a testament to the strong sense of community prevailing in the village. Visitors came and went, forging connections and offering a surrogate parenthood to the children. Drawing water from the spring was a routine task for the little girl, her water bottle rhythmically knocking against her knees. This endearing sight earned her the affectionate nickname "Congo Jug" among the villagers, who held her dear.

Living with her father, stepmother, and extended family, the young girl faced additional hardships. Her stepmother's abusive behaviour left scars both physical and emotional. At times, she resorted to feeding the girl cloth soaked in kerosene oil, a distressing practice that took a toll on the child's health. Nevertheless, her spirit remained unbroken, and her resilience shone through. One day, around the age of eight, her long-lost mother reappeared, bearing a precious gift: a pair of vibrant red ballet shoes. Overwhelmed with joy, the girl's heart swelled with hope and anticipation.

However, her mother's reappearance proved fleeting, leaving her longing for a connection that remained elusive. In this village, education took a backseat to farming, the primary source of income. The rich land yielded a bounty of tropical fruits, vegetables, sugar cane, and coconuts, attracting buyers from neighbouring villages. The village buzzed with activity, especially on market days when eager sellers prepared to catch the famous "Rugby Bus" that transported their goods.

Among the farmers, there was one renowned for his delectable sugarcane drink infused with lime and rum. Customers flocked to him, engaging in lively debates over the quantity they desired. Their enthusiasm added to the vibrant atmosphere of the village. Amidst the community's daily rhythm, the women gathered to harvest a special spice known as pimento. With its aromatic fragrance and distinctive flavour reminiscent of cinnamon, nutmeg, ginger, and cloves, pimento added a touch of magic to the village's culinary delights.

The women carefully dried and bagged the spice to sell, their collective efforts strengthening the bonds of friendship. The village river served as a gathering place, where women washed clothes and children revelled in the joy of swimming and play. These cherished moments brought laughter and respite, creating lasting memories of a childhood deeply intertwined with the rhythm of the village and the beginning of the journey into the little village, where resilience, love, and the vibrant tapestry of life weave together to create a story that will capture your heart.

Drawing water from the spring was a routine task for the little girl, her water bottle rhythmically knocking against her knees.

Chapter 2

Shadows of Betrayal

IN THE SENIOR girls' home, it was customary for the older girls to routinely assign household chores to the younger children, and they also became their unwilling servant. Each day, the staff would wake them up at the crack of dawn, around 5 am, signalling the start of a long and tiring routine. They were hurriedly bathed, dressed, and fed breakfast before embarking on the journey to school.

School brought temporary respite from the drudgery. But as the clock struck 3 pm, the end of classes marked the beginning of another phase. The children were granted a brief two-hour window to release their youthful energy through play. Laughter echoed through the halls as they revelled in their fleeting moments of joy. However, their blissful interlude would soon be interrupted by the call to return, signalling the end of their freedom.

It was time for baths, followed by the evening meal, and finally, the descent into sleep as the night blanketed the home. Fate had a different plan for this particular girl. She found herself entangled in the clutches of authority, her life thrown into turmoil as her case wound its way through the intricate web of the court system. The uncertainty weighed heavily on her, prolonging her stay in the suffocating environment. Days turned into weeks, weeks into months, as she anxiously awaited a resolution. Finally, after what felt like an eternity, the day arrived when she was granted release from the suffocating walls of the institution. The court recognised her aunt, who stood as a beacon of hope, as her temporary guardian. With mixed emotions of anticipation and apprehension, she stepped into a new chapter of her life.

As the days unfolded, the promise of a brighter

future began to fade. Within the confines of her aunt's care, she faced a different kind of hardship—abuse. The love and protection she longed for seemed to have vanished into thin air. Each passing day was a painful reminder of her vulnerability and the shattered trust she had once held. Desperate to escape the torment, she made a courageous decision to return to her father's house.

The familiar abode consisted of two houses within a shared yard. One was her father's dwelling, a humble two-room board house with a small shop attached. The other belonged to her blind grandfather, a single spacious room where the family would come together to sleep. Life at her father's house was a blend of fragments—a fragile mosaic of moments. In one room, a large bed and a smaller one stood, while the other room served as a makeshift dining area with a small bed tucked away. Her father, a hardworking man, would spend most of his time on the farm, where he had built a small dwelling for himself.

It was during one of their visits to the farm that a fateful event occurred, altering the course of her destiny. Her father entrusted her and her siblings with a simple task, to fetch cigarettes from a distant shop and return them to him. However, as darkness engulfed their path on the way back, panic seized their hearts. In a moment of desperation, they broke the cigarettes apart and discarded them among the bushes, hoping to erase any evidence of their delay.

Yet, fate has a way of revealing its secrets. Her father, upon returning home, stumbled upon the scattered remains of the cigarettes. Confronting her, he demanded answers she was too afraid to provide. Fear gripped her, and she uttered a lie, denying any knowledge of the cigarettes. But her father, his patience wearing thin, slowly opened his clenched hand, exposing the undeniable truth.

The weight of her deception came crashing down upon her. With rage consuming him, her father unleashed his anger upon her fragile frame. His hands became instruments of pain, and soon, he reached for a sturdy whisk, determined to teach her a harsh lesson. Blow after blow rained down upon her, leaving her bruised and broken. In her desperate bid for survival, she managed to escape his wrath, fleeing to the sanctuary of the family burial plot.

It was atop her sister's grave that she sought solace, finding a temporary refuge from the physical and emotional torment. For two agonising days, she remained hidden in the safety of her blind grandfather's house, nursing her wounds and nursing her shattered spirit.

The threads of her destiny continued to entwine, weaving a complex tapestry of struggle and resilience. Little did she know that this harrowing chapter was only the beginning of her journey. A journey that would test her strength, ignite her inner fire, and lead her to the realisation that the power to weave her own destiny lay within her own hands.

Laughter echoed through the halls as they revelled in their fleeting moments of joy.

Chapter 3

A Glimpse of Hope

AT THE TENDER age of 11, she mustered the courage to enrol herself in secondary school. However, she embarked on this journey barefoot, unable to afford a pair of shoes. The observant teachers noticed her lack of footwear and inquired about the reason. She candidly explained her situation, revealing that she did not possess any shoes. Concerned about her welfare, the teachers decided to follow her home after school to assess her living conditions.

Upon witnessing the impoverished environment, she called home, the school promptly involved the authorities. The little girl, once again, found herself in the clutches of authority. While their initial intention was to return her to the senior girls' home, a compassionate woman from the village intervened, offering her assistance and promising to ensure the girl's well-being.

Recognising the urgency of the situation, the authorities arranged for ongoing support and regular visits from school personnel and the police to monitor her progress. The little girl, relieved to have found temporary respite from her tumultuous past, began to rebuild her shattered dreams. At the age of 12, an unexpected visit changed her life once again. Her long-lost mother, who had been absent throughout her journey, appeared at the school. Overwhelmed with joy, the girl's heart swelled with excitement as she embraced her mother's arrival. Her mother shared the news that she had come to take her daughter home, to a place far different from the village she had known. This new area boasted modern amenities, such as water, electricity, beautiful houses, schools, and shops.

Her mother, a market vendor specialising in fish and other farm produce, had managed to carve out a better life for herself and her daughter. Eager to start a new life, the girl's mother wasted no time. Within weeks, she accompanied her daughter to a secondary school in the town area, enrolling her for further education. The school itself was nestled within lush farmland, surrounded by an array of fruit trees that provided a refreshing atmosphere for the children to enjoy during their breaks.

However, amidst the new beginnings, a shadow loomed over her happiness. A strict disciplinarian named Mr. Bull patrolled the school premises, his cane poised behind him. Any student caught outside their classroom during school hours would face his disciplinary actions. This fear consumed the girl to such an extent that she resorted to hiding in the nearby bushes instead of attending school for an entire week.

Concerned for her well-being, the school administration sent a letter home to her mother, revealing her absence and the reasons behind it. When her mother confronted her about the letter, the girl explained her crippling fear of Mr. Bull. However, her mother's reaction was far from understanding.

Consumed by anger, she subjected her daughter to a severe beating, leaving her body covered in painful bruises. This traumatic incident cast a dark shadow over their lives. Despite the challenges they faced, the girl and her mother continued to reside in the area for three more years before eventually moving to a different community. The transition marked a new phase in their journey, one filled with uncertainty but also the hope of a brighter future.

As the threads of destiny continued to weave their intricate patterns, the girl clung to the flickering flame of hope, yearning for stability, love, and a chance to rise above the adversities that had plagued her young life. Little did she know that the next chapter of her story would bring unexpected twists and turns, pushing her resilience to the brink and ultimately shaping her into the person she was destined to become.

Chapter 4

A Road to Redemption

WITH EACH PASSING day, the girl grew older, inching her way into her teenage years. Her mother's decision to move to a new village and live with her partner marked the beginning of a bittersweet chapter in their lives. The village, though remote and rural, possessed a captivating charm, boasting picturesque beaches and enchanting tourist attractions. Their humble abode, a two-room house reminiscent of her father's dwelling, became their sanctuary in this unfamiliar territory.

Little did she know that the path ahead would lead

her through the darkest depths of despair before offering a glimmer of hope and redemption. As she transitioned into her teenage years, the girl's world took a tragic turn, forever altering the course of her life. The stepfather, fuelled by his own twisted desires, approached her one day with a chilling proclamation: "No man shall enter this house." Unbeknownst to her, these words carried a sinister implication that would shatter the remnants of her innocence.

Her own uncle, taking advantage of his regular visits, succumbed to depravity and began subjecting her to unspeakable acts of sexual abuse. Trapped in a vortex of fear and shame, her voice silenced by the weight of secrets, she endured unspeakable torment. The days turned into a living nightmare, her innocence stripped away as trust and love crumbled before her eyes. Yet, fate, ever unpredictable, had a twisted turn in store. One fateful night, her stepfather stumbled upon the horrifying scene, catching her uncle in the act of violating her. A wave of anger and disgust washed over him, and he erupted in a fit of rage, berating the uncle for his unspeakable deeds.

In a chilling display of hypocrisy, the stepfather then unleashed the same monstrous actions upon her fragile being. It was a night of unimaginable horrors, one that would forever be etched in her memory. The following morning, as the sun timidly peeked through the curtains, the stepfather callously taunted her, revelling in his depravity. “You slept poorly last night; I had something thick in my hand,” he sneered, his words dripping with sadistic pleasure. The fire of defiance within her burned brighter than ever as she confronted him, hurling a storm of insults in response.

As soon as her mother returned home, the stepfather twisted the truth, weaving a web of deceit. He skilfully manipulated the events, painting the girl as the perpetrator rather than the victim. Consumed by her partner’s lies, her mother’s anger blazed like a wildfire, scorching the remnants of their shattered bond. In a cruel twist of fate, her mother cast her out, forcibly driving her away from the sanctuary she had once called home. Alone, betrayed, and desperate, the girl reached out to the one person she believed could provide solace and protection, her estranged father.

In an unexpected display of compassion, he responded to her plea for help, sending her money and urging her to pack her belongings. He assured her that she could find refuge in his embrace, a glimmer of hope in an otherwise bleak existence. With a heavy heart and a suitcase filled with shattered dreams, she embarked on a journey back to her father's house.

The road stretched before her, winding and treacherous, much like the path she had traversed throughout her tumultuous life. But within her, a flicker of determination burned, a fierce resolve to break free from the chains of her past and find the strength to rebuild her fractured spirit. Little did she know that this journey would mark the beginning of her liberation, an opportunity to rediscover her worth and reclaim her stolen innocence.

As she set foot on the path ahead, she vowed to never let the darkness of her past define her future. With newfound courage, she took her first step into the unknown, ready to face the challenges that awaited her with determination.

Chapter 5

Rising from Despair

ON ARRIVING IN the bustling city, the young girl was filled with excitement and anticipation. Her cousin introduced her to his friends and extended family, and for a while, she found solace in their company. However, as time passed, circumstances led her to move in with another family member. The house they lived in had limited space, forcing them to carry out their daily activities in the front yard. On one fateful Saturday, while she was washing clothes, chaos erupted. The air was filled with shouts and panicked screams, and people ran in every direction.

Startled, she dropped what she was doing and rushed inside the house. To her horror, a man with a menacing knife followed closely behind her. She let out a piercing scream, only to have her cries muffled as he forcefully covered her mouth. Helplessly, she endured a cruel assault, her innocence shattered in an instant. When her family members returned home and discovered her trembling in a corner, tears streaming down her face, they questioned her.

Yet, she remained silent, unable to find her voice to share the horrors she had endured. Days turned into weeks, and she locked herself inside the house, her heart heavy with sorrow. Despair overwhelmed her, and thoughts of death consumed her mind. In a moment of desperation, she decided to venture outside, seeking an escape from her unbearable pain. Fate guided her to a nearby factory, its sign advertising job opportunities. Summoning the last remnants of courage, she approached the security guard and inquired about the available positions.

To her surprise, he welcomed her and provided her with an application form. Although unfamiliar with the ways of the big city, she discovered numerous factories within walking distance of her new home. The garment factory she applied to called her for an interview, and she eagerly attended, drawing upon her limited sewing skills gained during her schooling years. The interview proved successful, and she secured a job in the factory, filled with a mix of relief and joy.

It offered a semblance of stability and a chance to rebuild her life. As she toiled away in the factory, she formed friendships with her co-workers. One day, a friend introduced her to a tall and handsome man on the factory floor, known as Bulldog. Initially sceptical, she found solace in his company, and a deep bond formed between them. Bulldog showed her kindness and care, even throwing her a birthday party, a luxury she had never experienced before. Their relationship flourished, and Bulldog asked her to move in with him.

Eager for a fresh start, she agreed, hoping that love would bring the happiness she craved. However, their joy was short-lived. Tragedy struck when she suffered a heart-breaking miscarriage three months into her pregnancy.

The loss devastated them both, but they clung to each other for support. In the midst of grief, a glimmer of hope emerged as she conceived once again. But this pregnancy brought forth a host of challenges, leaving her bedridden and in and out of hospitals. Overwhelmed, Bulldog urged her to terminate the pregnancy, unable to bear the hardships they faced.

She remained steadfast, refusing to let go of the life within her. In response, Bulldog made a heart-wrenching decision, he abandoned her, leaving her alone to navigate the treacherous journey ahead. With determination burning in her eyes, she emerged from the hospital, ready to face the trials that awaited her. Though the path was uncertain, she carried within her the strength of a phoenix rising from the ashes. This chapter marked her transformation, a testament to her resilience and indomitable spirit.

Chapter 6

The Unbreakable Spirit

THE YOUNG GIRL, now a single mother, found herself grappling with the weight of her newfound responsibilities. The days blurred together as she navigated the exhausting routine of caring for her infant son while striving to provide for their basic needs. It was a challenging juggling act, but she refused to let her circumstances define her. With her baby in day care during the day, she returned to work at the garment factory, where she had found solace amidst the chaos of her life.

The familiarity of the sewing machines and the

rhythmic hum of the factory floor offered her a respite from the hardships that had befallen her. She poured her heart and soul into her work, finding solace in the creativity and craftsmanship that sewing provided. As time passed, the young girl's dedication and talent caught the attention of her supervisors. They recognised her potential and offered her opportunities to take on more challenging projects. She eagerly accepted, embracing each task with determination and a drive to excel.

Her skills grew with every stitch she made, and she found a sense of pride in her craft. Within the walls of the factory, she formed bonds with her fellow co-workers, who became her second family. They shared stories of triumph and resilience, supporting one another through the trials and tribulations of their lives. Their camaraderie served as a beacon of hope, reminding her that she was not alone in her struggles.

Outside of work, the young girl dedicated herself to creating a nurturing and loving environment for her son. Though the weight of her past experiences still haunted her, she was determined to shield him from the pain she had endured. She filled their small home with laughter and love, cherishing each precious moment they shared together. As her son grew older, his curiosity and zest for life ignited a spark within her.

She realised that she wanted to provide him with every opportunity possible, to ensure that he could reach his full potential. With determination, she began to explore educational options for him, dreaming of a brighter future for her child. Meanwhile, the scars left by Bulldog's betrayal and her traumatic past continued to heal, albeit slowly. She sought solace in therapy and support groups, gradually unravelling the layers of pain and trauma that had accumulated over the years.

Through self-reflection and the guidance of compassionate professionals, she learned to redefine her worth and reclaim her sense of self. In the midst of her personal growth, a chance encounter introduced her to a kind-hearted individual who would become a steadfast presence in her life. Their friendship blossomed into something more, as they discovered a shared understanding of resilience and commitment to building a better future together.

With this newfound love and support, the young girl's journey took an unexpected turn. She found the strength to confront her past demons, to let go of the pain that had held her captive for so long. As she embarked on this path of healing and self-discovery, she realised that she had the power to shape her own destiny, to create a life filled with love, joy, and endless possibilities.

As the tables turn, it was a testament to the young girl's unbreakable spirit. Through the trials and tribulations, she faced, she refused to be defined by her past. Instead, she emerged as a resilient force, ready to embrace the future with open arms. This chapter marked a pivotal moment in her journey, as she learned to turn her pain into strength and seize control of her own happiness.

Chapter 7

Embracing Change

SEVEN YEARS HAD passed since the young girl embarked on her courageous journey, leaving behind her village and loved ones to seek a brighter future in a foreign land. This new chapter of her life unfolded with a mixture of anticipation and apprehension, as she set foot in an unfamiliar world filled with promises and uncertainties. As she settled into her new surroundings, the young girl soon figured that the path to a better life was not as smooth as she had envisioned. The foreign land presented its own set of challenges.

The weather, with its biting cold, was a stark contrast to the warmth of her homeland. She found herself yearning for the familiar sights and sounds that were now a distant memory. The initial excitement slowly waned as she faced one obstacle after another. Immigration processes proved to be a labyrinth of paperwork and bureaucracy, testing her patience and resolve. Finding stable accommodation became a daily struggle, and financial difficulties threatened to overshadow her dreams.

These trials weighed heavily on her spirit, and her health began to suffer under the strain. Yet, amidst the trials and tribulations, the young girl refused to succumb to despair. She clung to her faith, drawing strength from the promise of divine protection and guidance.

"Fear thou not; for I am with thee: be not dismayed; for I am thy God: I will strengthen thee; yea, I will help thee; yea, I will uphold thee with the right hand of my righteousness." Isaiah 41:10 (KJV)

This verse became her source of solace and inspiration, reminding her that she was not alone in her struggles. With each passing day, she mustered the courage to face the challenges head-on, determined to create a better life for herself and her child. In the midst of her journey, she discovered the power of education. Opportunities arose for her to pursue further learning and personal growth. Recognising the value of knowledge and skills, she eagerly enrolled in college.

Starting with foundational subjects like mathematics and English, she gradually expanded her studies to include health care assistance. The young girl's hunger for knowledge was insatiable. She thirsted for more, and with each lesson learned, her confidence grew. Eventually, she found herself delving into the field of health and social care for adults. It was a path that resonated deeply with her compassionate nature, igniting a newfound sense of purpose.

Returning to the classroom proved to be a transformative experience. Surrounded by fellow students from diverse backgrounds, she embraced the opportunity to learn and exchange ideas. The educational journey became a catalyst for personal growth, empowering her to envision a future where she could make a meaningful impact on the lives of others.

As the young girl immersed herself in her studies, she encountered remarkable individuals along the way—professors who nurtured her curiosity, classmates who became lifelong friends, and mentors who guided her through the intricacies of her chosen field. Their support and encouragement became the pillars upon which her dreams were built.

With each milestone achieved, she began to feel the winds of change blowing in her favour. The hardships she endured started to bear fruit as doors of opportunity gradually opened before her. The resilience that had carried her through the darkest moments now propelled her towards the light at the end of the tunnel.

Chapter 8

A Journey of Healing

AS THE SUN rises on a new chapter in the young girl's life, she finds herself standing at the precipice of transformation and healing. The journey of healing invites us to witness the remarkable events that unfold as she navigates the challenges with strength and determination.

In the wake of her ongoing struggles with physical and mental health, a ray of hope illuminates her path as she is referred for psychological counselling. Stepping into the counselling room, she embarks on a voyage of self-discovery, confronting the deep-seated wounds that have shaped her journey thus far. With the guidance of her compassionate therapist, she learns to navigate the intricacies of her emotions, embracing healing as she sheds the weight of past traumas.

Simultaneously, her friends from church and Christian groups provide support, reminding her of her inherent worth and encouraging her to forge ahead. However, the road to healing takes an unexpected turn when a medical error robs her of her eyesight. In the darkness that engulfs her world, she reaches out to her faith community for solace and strength. United in prayer, they beseech the divine for restoration, believing in the miraculous power of God. Their collective faith is rewarded as a newfound light dawn upon her, and her vision is miraculously restored. Filled with gratitude and a deepened sense of purpose, she emerges from this trial with a renewed perspective on life.

Yet, the journey is far from over. The young girl faces yet another daunting challenge as she receives a diagnosis of kidney failure. For five arduous years, she undergoes the gruelling regimen of dialysis, battling against the physical and emotional toll it takes on her. But hope flickers within her heart, igniting a flame of determination that refuses to be extinguished. On a poignant Father's Day celebration, a phone call alters the course of her destiny. A suitable kidney donor has been found, presenting her with a lifeline and a renewed lease on life.

Brimming with excitement and gratitude, she enters the operating room, placing her trust in the skilled hands of medical professionals. The transplant is a resounding success, and as she emerges from the haze of anaesthesia, she takes her first breaths with a renewed sense of purpose. In the aftermath of her successful transplant, the young girl embarks on a year of profound transformation and growth. Empowered by her second chance at life, she resolves to embrace a healthier lifestyle, nurturing her body, mind, and soul.

With newfound vigour, she adopts a balanced diet, engages in regular exercise, and explores holistic practices that promote overall well-being. Inspired by her own experiences, she sets her sights on a new goal: becoming a social worker. Fuelled by her desire to support and uplift others who have faced similar hardships, she immerses herself in studies and embarks on a path of professional development. Alongside her academic pursuits, she dedicates her time to volunteering within her community, offering a helping hand and a listening ear to those in need.

Through her encouragement and compassionate guidance, she becomes a beacon of hope, inspiring others to persevere and find their own paths to healing and fulfilment. The young girl's journey of healing stands as a testament to the power of resilience, faith, and the unwavering human spirit. Through the depths of darkness and the triumphs of light, she emerges as a transformed individual, armed with a deep sense of purpose and a profound understanding of the value of every thread woven into the fabric of her destiny.

Chapter 9

Victory Over Adversity

As we witness the triumph of the young girl's indomitable spirit over the adversities that once threatened to consume her. Having weathered the storms of life, she emerges as a beacon of hope and resilience. No longer defined by her past struggles, she has forged a path of triumph against all odds. Now a qualified commis chef, she brings her passion for culinary arts to life, showcasing her talent and creativity in the kitchen. Through her culinary endeavours, she finds solace and joy, turning her passion into a vessel for self-expression and healing.

In addition to her culinary pursuits, she also dedicates her time and energy to serve her community in various capacities. With a heart full of compassion, she takes on the role of moderating prayer sessions, providing guidance and support to those seeking solace and spiritual nourishment. Furthermore, she becomes an integral part of the welfare department in the Unique Women's organisation, extending love and care to vulnerable individuals in need.

Through these acts of service, she embraces her purpose, weaving threads of kindness and empathy into the lives of others. Against all odds, the young girl defies the limitations that once threatened to confine her. In a testament to her incredible strength, she accomplishes a remarkable feat—a 10k marathon walk. Just five years prior, she had been told that she may never walk or use her hands again. Her triumphant walk not only showcases her physical resilience but also serves as a symbolic victory over the adversity that once sought to hold her back.

It is a shining testament to the power of perseverance and the boundless possibilities that lie within the human spirit. The young girl's metamorphosis from a survivor to a thriver, from a victim of circumstances to an empowered individual, unfolds in "Threads of Destiny." Her journey of overcoming adversity and embracing her true potential serves as an inspiration to all who face their own trials and tribulations.

It is a celebration of the extraordinary triumphs that can be achieved when one chooses to rise above their circumstances and embrace the limitless possibilities that life has to offer. Embracing the Warrior within is a testament to the young girl's remarkable spirit and her remarkable ability to rise above adversity. It serves as a clarion call to embrace the warrior that resides within each of us, to confront our fears, and to unleash our full potential.

As we near the final chapter of her extraordinary journey, we eagerly anticipate the culmination of her triumph, where she emerges as a shining example of the heights that can be reached when one fully embraces their inner warrior. Her story is a testament to the indomitable spirit that resides within each of us, reminding us that through resilience, determination, and belief, we have the power to overcome any obstacle and achieve greatness.

In a testament to her incredible strength, she accomplishes a remarkable feat — a 10k marathon walk.

Chapter 10

Testimonies of Triumph

IN THE RESOUNDING conclusion of "Threads of Destiny: A Village Girl's Tale," the voices of those who have been touched by Maria Bell's extraordinary journey unite in a chorus of testimonies, each echoing the resiliency of the human spirit.

Elizabeth, a steadfast friend who witnessed Maria's determination, shares her heartfelt testimony: *"I have had the privilege of walking alongside Maria for many years, witnessing her incredible strength in the face of adversity. Through the ups and downs of her health battles, she remained steadfast, finding the courage to keep going. Her faith and gratitude have inspired me beyond words."*

Rev. Praise Asemota nee Sam-Jolly, deeply moved by Maria's faith, adds: *"Maria's journey is a testament to the power of faith. She has faced immense hardships, yet she has never wavered in her belief that God has a plan for her life. Her trust in the face of uncertainty is a shining example of what it means to walk by faith."*

May, a close friend of Maria shares her encounter: *"I had the privilege of meeting Maria a couple of years ago when she was going to dialysis three times a week. As a close friend who shared different accommodations with her, I had a first-hand view of how profoundly it affected her life. Despite the challenges, Maria's faith shone brightly, inspiring those around her. There were moments when she would break down, as any human would, but each time, she picked herself up with remarkable strength. I recall a time when her health deteriorated to the point where I had to lend a helping hand in her personal care, and witnessing her resilience and determination during that period filled me with immense pride. Today, I stand in awe of the woman she has become, a beacon of hope and inspiration to us all".*

In the midst of Maria's incredible journey, Kemi also witnessed the strength of Maria's character and the depth of her faith. She adds:

"As Maria released her book, two emotions flooded my heart – overwhelming joy and deep gratitude. I couldn't contain my happiness, witnessing her dream become a reality, transforming her life from a mere story to one of glory. From the first time I met her until now, her journey to becoming a published author is nothing short of a miracle.

Maria's trust, faith, and gratitude in God's words are truly exceptional. The saying;

"Life is peaceful when you rest on the promises of God's word. Proved to be true throughout her battle with kidney problems, her favorite verse, "If you believe it, you will receive it" (Matthew 21:22), has been a source of strength and thanksgiving. Her life testimonies clearly demonstrate that God's words are indeed faithful and true. In the face of life's rough and tough challenges, Maria never allowed herself to be overwhelmed.

Instead, she stood tall, firmly anchored in the promises of her Creator. Despite doctors' diagnoses, prognoses, and complications, Maria's faith remained solid, keeping her standing strong. I am confident that Maria's book will touch countless lives, providing encouragement and guiding many towards the saving grace and knowledge of Christ Jesus.

Her positive mindset, coupled with her commitment to spiritual guidance, diet, exercise, and more, serves as a powerful inspiration to everyone who reads her story. Personally, I cannot wait to dive into the pages of Maria's life testimonies. Her journey is a testament to the power of faith and the incredible strength that comes from trusting in God's promises. With every turn of the page, I know I will be uplifted and encouraged, just as I have been by knowing her".

These testimonies, intertwined with Maria's own narrative, paint a vivid picture of resilience and triumph. They highlight the profound impact she has had on those around her, serving as a beacon of hope and inspiration. In this final chapter, we invite you to bear witness to the collective echoes of resilience that reverberate throughout Maria's story. Through the voices of those who have been touched by her indomitable spirit, you will be uplifted and inspired to face your own challenges with determination.

As you read the final pages of "Threads of Destiny: A Village Girl's Tale," may the testimonies of triumph embedded within them ignite a spark within you. Let Maria's journey remind you that you too, possess the strength to overcome any obstacle and redefine your own destiny. Embrace the power of faith, resilience, and the overcoming spirit that resides within each of us. Allow the echoes of resilience to guide you on your own journey of self-discovery and triumph.

In closing this chapter, we honour Maria's courage and celebrate the transformative power of resilience. May her story continue to inspire generations to come, echoing through time as a testament to the extraordinary heights that can be reached when we choose to embrace our own strength and rise above life's greatest challenges. Echoes of resilience linger in the air, reminding us that no matter the circumstances we face, we can rise, we can overcome, and we can shape our own destiny.

A Village Girl's Tale,
may the testimonies of
triumph embedded within
them ignite a spark
within you.

Chapter 11

Conclusion

REFLECTING ON THE remarkable journey, we have traversed through the pages of this book, it becomes evident why Maria's determination and empowerment drives her to share her story and transform lives. Despite the challenging circumstances life has dealt her, Maria has emerged as one of the most blessed and enriched individuals. Not many would have survived, let alone found the strength to tell their own story.

Yet, Maria stands as a living testimony, breathing out words of encouragement to those who may be on the brink of giving up, assuring them that tomorrow holds the promise of a brighter future. For those who find themselves in the depths of despair, convinced that life has dealt them an insurmountable blow, Maria wants you to know that you are worthy and needed. You are precious, and your presence in this world is invaluable.

Through her own journey of resilience, she implores you to hold onto hope, for it is the beacon that can guide you out of the darkest of ditches. Each day brings the opportunity for transformation and renewal. Embrace it with open arms and a steadfast belief that better days lie ahead.

As we conclude this transformative journey, carry with you the following empowering words of affirmation and quotes that serve as guiding lights on our own paths.

"Believe in yourself and all that you are. Know that there is something inside you that is greater than any obstacle."

Christian D. Larson

"Every setback is a setup for a comeback."

Joel Osteen

"The greatest glory in living lies not in never falling, but in rising every time we fall."

Nelson Mandela

"Believe you can and you're halfway there."

Theodore Roosevelt

"Your present circumstances don't determine where you can go; they merely determine where you start."

Nido Qubein

"You may encounter many defeats, but you must not be defeated. In fact, it may be necessary to encounter the defeats, so you can know who you are, what you can rise from, how you can still come out of it."

Maya Angelou

"Hardships often prepare ordinary people for an extraordinary destiny."

C.S. Lewis

Words of Affirmations

- *I am stronger than I believe, braver than I seem, and more capable than I know.*
- *I am grateful for all the blessings in my life*
- *I am strong and capable of overcoming any challenge*
- *I am living a life of purpose and fulfilment*
- *I embrace my journey, for it is shaping me into the person I am meant to become.*
- *I am a masterpiece in progress, constantly evolving and growing stronger with each challenge I overcome.*
- *My past does not define my future. I have the power to create a new story for myself.*

May these quotes and words of affirmation inspire you to embrace your own journey of resilience, to believe in your inherent worthiness, and to seize the limitless possibilities that lie before you. Remember, you are the author of your own story, and your narrative has the power to impact and inspire others. With every step forward, you contribute to the beautiful tapestry of human resilience and the triumph of the human spirit.